CHATPATI

Nita Mehta's

CHAAT

100% TRIED & TESTED RECIPES

Nita Mehta

B.Sc. (Home Science), M.Sc. (Food and Nutrition) Gold Medalist

Tanya Mehta

SNAB
Excellence in Books

Nita Mehta's
Chatpati
CHAAT
© Copyright 2005-2010 **SNAB** Publishers Pvt Ltd

5th Print 2010
ISBN 978-81-7869-089-6

Food Styling and Photography: **SNAB** Excellence in Books

Layout and Laser Typesetting :

National Information Technology Academy
3A/3, Asaf Ali Road
New Delhi-110002
☎ 23252948

Published by :

SNAB Excellence in Books
Publishers Pvt. Ltd.
3A/3 Asaf Ali Road, New Delhi - 110002
Tel: 23252948, 23250091

Contributing Writers :
Anurag Mehta
Tanya Mehta
Subhash Mehta

Editors :
Sangeeta
Sunita

Editorial and Marketing office:
E-159, Greater Kailash-II, N.Delhi-48
Fax: 91-11-29225218, 29229558
Tel: 91-11-29214011, 29218574
E-Mail: nitamehta@email.com
✉ nitamehta@nitamehta.com
Website: http://www.nitamehta.com
Website: http://www.snabindia.com

Distributed by :

NITA MEHTA BOOKS
3A/3, Asaf Ali Road, New Delhi - 02

Distribution Centre:
D16/1, Okhla Industrial Area, Phase-I, New Delhi-110020
Tel.: 26813199, 26813200
Bhogal: Tel.: 24372279

Printed by :

MEHTA OFFSET

Recipe Development & Testing:

Nita Mehta Classes/Foods
3A/3, Asaf Ali Road, New Delhi-110002
E-143, Amar Colony, Lajpat Nagar-IV
New Delhi-110024

Rs. 89/-

INTRODUCTION

It's tasty! It's tangy! What is it that we are talking about? Chaat!!!

Almost every Indian is familiar with this delicacy called chaat. It is sold on the street and enjoyed by most people. Now you can enjoy the same flavour and taste, sitting in the comfort of your home. This cookbook has recipes of the tastiest and the tangiest chaats available throughout the country.

We visited the local streets of many cities and asked the hawkers to share their secrets for authentic chaat recipes. We have suitably adapted the recipes, keeping in mind the growing awareness towards healthy eating.

The book includes the popular recipes like Sev Puri, Golgappa, Tikki etc. There is a section of unusual chaats like Kurkura Chaat, Palak Pakoda Chaat etc. which will surely surprise you.

Now, call your friends over and surprise them with your home cooked chaat.

Nita Mehta

ABOUT THE RECIPES

WHAT'S IN A CUP?

INDIAN CUP
1 teacup = 200 ml liquid
AMERICAN CUP
1 cup = 240 ml liquid (8 oz.)
The recipes in this book were tested with the Indian teacup which holds 200 ml liquid.

CONTENTS

Dilli ke Raste Ki Chaat   33

Mumbai Chowpati Chaat   57

Chaat Kuch Alag !! 74

Chatpati Chutneys 96

Ab Kuch Meetha 101

Tips on Chaats

- All chaats should be prepared at the time of serving.
- Papadis (puris) and golgappas can be made well in advance. Store papadis and golgappas in an air tight jar. It lasts upto a month.
- Sev, murmuras and pav are easily available ready-made in packets. So are papadis and golgappas, but still I have given the recipes for home-made papadis and golgappas.
- Always use **Bhuna Jeera Powder (roasted cumin powder)** for chaats. To make bhuna jeera powder, heat a tawa on fire. Put ½ cup jeera on it. Stir continuously on low heat till jeera starts to change colour and turns fragrant. Let it turn golden brown. Remove to a plate immediately. When it cools down, grind to a rough powder in a small mixer/spice grinder. Store for a month in an air tight bottle.
- You can increase the spiciness of chaats according to your own taste.
- Top any chaat with fresh pomegranate seeds (annar ke daane). It tastes good. It also enhances the look of any chaat.
- Imli chutney can be made and stored in a bottle in the fridge and for longer duration it can also be stored in the freezer.

Chaat Pakodi

Dahi Papadi

Picture on cover   *Serves 5 (25 puris)*

Most popular streetside chaat which is simple to make but yet so delicious.

DOUGH FOR PAPADI/PURI
1 cup maida (flour), 1 cup wheat flour (atta)
2 tsp oil, ½ cup water, oil for frying

TOPPING
2 medium potatoes - boiled and chopped
3 tbsp boiled channas (safed chhole)
1 tsp chaat masala
1 tsp bhuna jeera powder (roasted cumin seed powder)
1 tsp red chilli powder, salt to taste
some hari chutney (given on page 97)
some saunth or quick meethi chutney (see page 98 or 99)

MIX TOGETHER
2 cups fresh curd, 5- 6 tsp sugar, ½ tsp salt, ½ cup water

GARNISH
1" piece of ginger - cut into thin matchsticks
2 tbsp fresh pomegranate seeds (annar ke daane)

1. To prepare the papadi/puris, mix maida and wheat flour. Add oil and rub with the finger tips. Add just enough water to make a stiff dough. Knead well till smooth.
2. Roll out small thin puris of 2" diameter.
3. Prick them 2 to 3 times with a fork.
4. Heat oil in a kadhai. Fry puris on low heat until light brown. Keep aside.
5. Mix dahi with all the ingredients written under mix together in a bowl. Beat well.
6. Arrange papadis in a serving plate.
7. Top with the potatoes, channas and mixed curd.
8. Pour saunth and green chutney in circles over the curd.
9. Sprinkle chaat masala, cumin seed powder and red chilli powder on top. Serve immediately garnished with ginger matchsticks and anaar ke daane (optional).

Golgappas/Pani Puri

Popularly known as Golgappas in Delhi and pani puri in Bombay. Puchka is another name for it. Golgappas are stuffed with potatoes and served with poodina pani. It's delicious.

Picture on cover   *Serves 4*

DOUGH FOR THE GOLGAPPAS/PURIS
½ cup suji (fine), ½ cup maida (plain flour)

1. Mix suji and maida and knead a stiff dough with about ¼ cup water. Cover dough with wet muslin cloth and keep aside for 2 hours.
2. Take tiny marble sized balls of dough and roll each into thin puris of 1½" diameter.
3. Heat oil in a kadhai and fry puris immediately. (puri should not get dry). Keep the dough covered while rolling out puris. Fry puris on low heat, turning twice till just golden brown. Store puris in an air tight container after they turn cold.

FILLING
1 large potato - boiled & chopped, ½ cup boiled safed chhole - boiled some saunth or quick meethi chutney (see page 98 or 99)

POODINA PANI

50 gm poodina or mint leaves (2 bunches)
2 tbsp fresh coriander leaves
1 green chilli, juice of one lemon
2 tsp black salt (kala namak), 1½ tsp salt
1 tsp jeera (cumin seeds)
7-8 saboot kali mirch (black peppercorns)
½ tsp saunf (fennel seeds)

1. Grind all the ingredients of poodina pani to a fine paste.
2. Add 2 cups of water to this paste and mix well. Chill pani.
3. To serve, make a hole in the centre of a puri, fill some boiled safed chhole and potato. Add a spoonful of imli chutney and fill it with poodina pani. Eat immediately.

Note: To make puris, you might get tempted to roll out a big round and then cut into smaller rounds with a sharp lid or a biscuit cutter. But this will not work. Although it is going to take longer, each puri has to be rolled individually.

Bhel Puri

Stir up this chaat any time in the evening and your family will love it. But remember to make it fresh and serve it immediately!

Picture on backcover   *Serves 3-4*

2 cups murmura (puffed rice)
4-5 papadis - roughly break into pieces (buy ready-made or see page 12)
2 tsp roasted peanuts (moongphali) - split into 2 with a chakla belan
1 small potato - boiled and chopped
1 small onion - chopped finely
1-2 green chillies - remove seeds and chop finely
1 tsp chaat masala, ¼ tsp kala namak
2 tbsp hari chutney (see page 97)
3- 4 quick meethi chutney (see page 98 or 99)
1 tbsp red garlic chutney (given on next page)

GARNISH
1-2 tbsp chopped green coriander
4 tbsp fine namkeen sev (ready-made)

1. Dry roast the murmura (puffed rice) in a kadhai for 10 minutes on medium flame, stirring continuously, but do not let it turn brown. This makes the murmura crunchy and crisp.
2. Combine all the ingredients in a large bowl mixing. Mix well.
3. Serve immediately garnished with coriander and fine sev namkeen.

Red Garlic Chutney:

Soak peeled flakes of 1 whole pod garlic with 6-8 dried red chillies in 1 cup warm water for 15 minutes. Drain and blend them with 1 tbsp of vinegar to a paste. Add enough water for grinding to get a chutney consistency. Add salt to taste.

Tikki

Picture on facing page   *Serves 8*

5 medium (600 gm) potatoes - boiled and mashed
2 tbsp cornflour, 1 tsp salt, ½ tsp baking powder
5-6 tbsp ghee or oil for shallow frying

FILLING

½ cup dhuli moong dal (split, skinned green beans)
½ tsp jeera (cumin seed), 2 pinches hing (asafoetida)
½" piece ginger - finely chopped, 1 green chilli - finely chopped
1 tsp dhania powder, ½ tsp red chilli powder, ½ tsp chaat masala
½ tsp garam masala, 1 tbsp coriander leaves - chopped, ½ tsp salt

ACCOMPANIMENT

some saunth or quick meethi chutney (see page 98 or 99)

1. For the filling, soak dal overnight or for at least for 3-4 hours in water,
    keeping the water 2" above the dal. Drain dal and grind in a mixer to
    a rough paste. Do not grind too much, you should be able to see some
    whole dal grains in the dal paste. Grind for a few seconds only. Push

Contd...